IN

Geography

THE BEST TEST PAPER BLUNDERS

Richard Benson

summersdale

F IN GEOGRAPHY

Summersdale Publishers Ltd
46 West Street
Chichester
West Sussex
PO19 1RP
UK

www.summersdale.com

Printed and bound in China

ISBN: 978-1-84953-325-6

Substantial discounts on bulk quantities of Summersdale books are available to corporations, professional associations and other organisations. For details telephone Summersdale Publishers on (+44-1243-771107), fax (+44-1243-786300) or email (nicky@summersdale.com).

Contents

Introduction

Did your Geography exams involve confusion between your Andes and your Pyrenees? Thousands of people have relived their exam-day nightmares with *F in Exams*, and we just couldn't resist bringing you some more hilarious test paper blunders in this bite-size Geography edition.

This book is full to the brim with funny answers from clueless but canny students of geography which will have you cackling at continental drift, chuckling at climate, and howling hysterically at human geography. Just don't blame us if your geography teacher sends you on a one-way trip to the naughty corner…

Subject: **Climates & Environments**

Where can you find the Andes?

Google Earth.

What is the difference between biotic and abiotic factors in an ecosystem?

A.

What methods are used for preserving rainforest?

Pickling

What is afforestation?

when the train stops in the forests.

ⱲⱲⱲ

Why can flooding be beneficial?

If you're on fire

Describe two negative effects of a drought.

1. No swimming

2. No wet T-shirt competitions.

Where are temperate deciduous forests found?

In places that are not too hot or cold.

What are plants that are able to store water called?

clever.

Where are deserts found?

In the chilled
aisle

What is salinisation?

Cleaning.

What does the term 'glaciation' refer to?

A FOOD PROCESS —
E.G. GLACIATED CHERRIES.

What is the name for the long lakes found at the bottom of deep glacial valleys?

Geoff & Harry.

Name one cause of avalanches.

Yodelling

14

How are sedimentary rocks formed?

That's sedimentary, my dear Watson.

Photos of the Alps show that glaciers have retreated over the last 50 years. One reason for this could be climate change. What could another reason be?

They're shy.

Describe the greenhouse effect.

When you get old and spend all your time in the greenhouse, tending plants.

Why is it helpful to leave dead wood to rot?

Because if you use it to build things it breaks.

What were the main exports of Persia?

Cats and rugs

Turkey has seen a fall in its levels of export trade. Give one possible reason for this.

A rise in vegetarianism — turkeys being eaten less.

What does a choropleth map show?

location of choropleths.

Where would you find the Pyrenees?

In the mountains.

Everest base camp is an example of an extreme environment visited by tourists. Give two reasons why tourists visit extreme environments.

1. They didn't read the brochure
2. They want to impress their friends

Give two reasons people would visit Iceland.

1. Cheap food
2. Good advertising.

What is meant by a 'fragile environment'?

A glass house

Why do people continue to live in areas affected by tropical storms?

Good schools, off-road parking, quiet neighbours.

Subject: ......**The Coast & Rivers**......

What does it mean if a waterfall has an overhang?

Not enough exercise, too many chips

What is the hydrological cycle also known as?

Clever water bike.

How much of the world's water is stored in seas and oceans?

A LOT.

What is the drainage basin?

A sink without a plug.

What is a confluence?

When two things happen at the same time, unexpectedly.

What is the mouth of a river?

It is how the river eats.

What is an oxbow lake?

A lake protected by a cow that's good at archery.

What is the watershed?

Where fish do DIY.

Describe the process of abrasion.

It's a way to cook steak.

What is created when a river runs over alternating layers of hard and soft rock?

Glam rock.

Name one key force of change in a coastal system.

THE R.N.L.I.

How are waves created?

1. Lift your arm.
2. Shake your hand
   back and forth.

What is the distance a wave has travelled called?

The sea.

When does a constructive wave occur?

When I do well on sports day and mum waves and shouts 'well done'.

When is deposition likely to occur?

When you are at the bank

What are wooden barriers built at right-angles to the beach called?

fences.

What is it called when areas of coastline are allowed to erode and then flood naturally?

Laziness

What is a storm surge?

When the gods get angry.

Name a way of protecting a coastal area from flooding.

Armed police

What is the direction of longshore drift?

UP.

There are many different ways in which the sea erodes the coast. Explain two ways in which the sea erodes the coast.

1. Nibbling
2. Biting

Describe one key difference between destructive and constructive waves.

Constructive waves are constructive. Destructive waves are destructive.

Explain the causes of cliff recession along the
UK coastline.

*Nobody will pay to see him
any more, not even in
Blackpool.*

Some people agree with the building of coastal
defences while others disagree with it. Why is
this?

*Some people will disagree
with anything.*

What is the purpose of dams?

Similar to blast and gah.

What is a groyne?

A noise of pain.

Subject: **How the Earth Works**

What environmental factors can cause plate slippage?

Loose table legs.

What is slumping?

Bad posture.

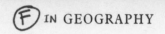

How old is the Earth?

Years.

What do the geological time periods relate to?

We have geography at 11am on Wednesdays and Fridays.

Which part of the Earth is directly below the crust?

The filling

Describe the different phases of the rock cycle.

It developed from Rythym and Blues and Jazz, into Rock'n'Roll and then into Rock.

What is the more common name for kaolin?

Ninja.

Name a characteristic of metamorphic rock.

Changeable.

Name a characteristic of igneous rock.

Very clever.

Which part of the Earth is the hottest?

Africa.

Give two differences between continental crust and oceanic crust.

One is on French pizza, the other is on seafood pizza.

How are fold mountains formed?

Origami.

What causes earthquakes?

Volcanoes.

Give two ways in which people can be prepared for earthquakes.

1. HOLD ON TIGHT.
2. GET IN A ZORBING BALL.

What is the name for professionals who monitor and predict volcanic eruptions?

Vulcans

Give an example of a supervolcano.

Describe the likely worldwide effects of a supervolcano eruption.

Death.
Dinosaurs.

What is a tsunami?

a move in
Sumo wrestling

What is the name for the scientific practice of studying the atmosphere and monitoring and predicting the weather and climate?

Being a weatherman.

Where do hurricanes normally form?

In the air.

Which part of the British Isles experiences the shortest days during the winter and the longest days during the summer?

France

What is meant by extreme weather?

When you have to stay indoors

December 2010 is one example of extreme weather in the UK. What was December 2010 a period of?

Winter

Draw an annotated diagram to explain the process of relief rainfall.

How does temperature differ at a high altitude, compared to temperature at a low altitude?

It's higher at high altitudes and lower at low altitudes.

What does the term latitude refer to?

It's French for attitude

Subject: Human Geography One
Urban Life & Systems

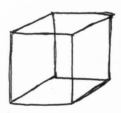

What public services does a youthful population put a strain on?

Beer
Traffic cones
Shopping trollies

What is a disadvantage of nuclear power?

The people who own it might get power crazy.

Explain the increase in demand for water and electricity in the south of England.

They're thirsty and keep getting bigger TVs.

Why does population naturally change over time?

It gets bored.

Describe two ways of reducing the demand for water.

1. When it's yellow let it mellow
2. When it's brown flush it down.

What is meant by the term 'carbon footprint'?

Someone who steps in soot has them.

What tends to happen to a country's carbon footprint as it develops?

IT GETS DARKER.

What does feedback in an industrial system involve?

A loud, high-pitched noise.

What is secondary industry?

Not as good as
primary industry.

Which sector employs the most people in the
UK?

The job sector.

Name a factor which might attract a multinational corporation to a country.

Nice beaches.

What is it called when a foreign country invests in a country?

Investment

Name a negative impact of globalisation.

You can never see the bits at the top and bottom where the frame goes:

Name two economic indicators.

Left blinker and right blinker.

What does the term population distribution refer to?

The spread of fizzy drinks throughout the country.

What is meant by population density?

How stupid people are.

How many people could there be on the planet by 2025?

None – the world will end in 2017

Describe one major problem caused by counter-urbanisation.

The urbanisers might get angry.

What is a 'migrant'?

A really bad headache.

Migration from a country may have both positive and negative effects. Describe these effects.

Positive- Moving somewhere nice
Negative- Moving somewhere horrible

Describe some ways that pollution problems could be reduced in cities in poorer parts of the world.

Get rid of the cows.

What does CBD stand for?

Currently Bored Dizzy

Explain why the number of food miles is increasing.

PEOPLE DEMAND FREE-RANGE, SO THE CHICKENS RUN MORE MILES EVERY DAY.

What is GNP?

A far right
political party

Many countries now have an ageing
population. Give two problems which may be
caused by an ageing population.

Shortage of light blue hair dye.
Longer queues on pension day.

Subject: **Human Geography Two**
Rural Life & Sustainability

What is a nucleated village?

One that's close to a nuclear
power station.

What factors affect the sustainability of food
sources?

How much people like the
taste of them.

Describe reasons for the change in the rural-urban fringe.

Drunken haircuts.

Describe the process of irrigation.

When a farmer irritates his crops they grow faster

Which type of feature is Watlowes an example of?

A cut-price supermarket.

Give a reason for the decline in employment in primary and secondary industries in the UK.

Less children.

Name one advantage of quarrying.

Any disagreements are out in the open and can be dealt with.

Name one disadvantage of quarrying.

Sometimes it ends in tears, or blows.

Name one way in which the impact of quarrying can be reduced.

Softer hammers.

What can a quarry be used for after the rock has been extracted?

Film sets.

What is a brownfield site?

A site with no grass, just mud.

Explain the terms 'subsistence farming' and 'nomadic farming'.

One is underground and the other is done by gnomes.

Give one positive aspect of organic farming.

The organic labels look prettier

What is meant by 'pull' and 'push' factors?

How strong the teams are in a tug of war.

What is meant by 'factory farming'?

Growing factories.

What is 'agri-business'?

A bad way of running your business as you might lose customers.

What is the difference between 'hard' and 'soft' engineering techniques?

The consistency.

The tourist industry has grown rapidly during the last 50 years. Give reasons for this rapid growth.

More tourists

Describe the characteristics of shanty houses.

1. Near the seaside
2. Full of people who like singing

The development of greenfield sites can threaten the countryside. Explain why this can be the case.

Greenfield sites are
very aggressive.

What is urbanisation?

More people listening
to R'n'B.

Explain two possible causes of rural depopulation.

1. No-one fancies farmers
2. People leave because the countryside smells funny.

What is meant by 'the development gap'?

The time it takes for you to get your photos back from the shop!

 IN GEOGRAPHY

Explain the difference between standard of living and quality of life.

It's the difference between home brand cola and the real thing.

What is 'stewardship'?

Difficult times for beef stews, lamb stews etc.

What is meant by the term ecotourism?

Travelling to Bognor Regis by coach.

If you're interested in finding out more about our humour books, follow us on Twitter:
@SummersdaleLOL

www.summersdale.com